PREFACE TO THE 4TH EDI

GW00420234

The Royal Canal has changed har
waterway - the Royal Canal C
Navigation, the New Royal Canal (
Company, Great Southern Railways
the Waterways Service of the Depa
This chequered history helped to ensure that the canal was never the commercial success that it might have been. It also helped to foster the widely-
held view that the canal had no role in modern Ireland. Today, however, the
future for the Royal Canal is brighter than at almost any time in its past.

The restoration of the canal was begun in 1974 by the Royal Canal Amenity
Group (RCAG) with the co-operation of CIE. When The Office of Public Works
took over the canal in 1986 the restoration programme was expanded and
accelerated. By 1990 the 46 mile (74 km) stretch between Blanchardstown
and Mullingar was navigable. The Waterways Service dredgers have now
reached Lock 45. By Spring 1997 breast gates and tail gates will have been
fitted in all lock chambers from Lock 1 in Dublin to Lock 38 beyond
Ballynacargy. Full restoration of the canal from the River Liffey to the River
Shannon is expected to be completed by the turn of the century.

The RCAG is still as active as ever, and do invaluable work through volunteers
and social employment schemes - clearing towpaths, constructing slipways,
developing amenity areas. Their help and co-operation over the years has
done much to raise the profile of the Royal Canal, and to make restoration
to full navigation a viable option for this long-neglected waterway.

This edition of the **Guide to the Royal Canal** is based on earlier editions
produced by the Inland Waterways Association of Ireland (IWAI). The
Waterways Service has now taken over the responsibility for this publication,
and is indebted to the IWAI for its commitment over the years. In particular
we would like to thank Ian Bath and Ruth Delany for their help in preparing
this guide. The text has been updated and the maps enhanced for this edition, which takes into account all the developments along the canal since
1994 when the guide was last published.

Waterways Service 1997

CONTENTS:

Produced By The Waterways Service with the co-operation of the Inland
Waterways Association of Ireland

Typesetting & Maps: ERA-Maptec Ltd., 36 Dame Street, Dublin 2.
Tel:+353-1-679 9227

Disclaimer: While every effort has been made to ensure accuracy in the
information supplied, no responsibility can be accepted for any damage or
loss suffered as a result of error, omission or misinterpretation of this information

GENERAL INFORMATION

The Royal Canal is administered by the Waterways Service of the Department of Arts, Culture and the Gaeltacht, 51 St. Stephen's Green, Dublin 2. Tel: 01-661 3111.

The Main Line of the canal is 90.5 miles (145.6 km) long with 46 locks (10 double chambered). In addition there is a sea lock where the canal joins the River Liffey in Dublin, but this is no longer in use, the canal being tidal as far as the 1st lock beyond Spencer Dock (see page 5). The Longford Branch is 5.2 miles (8.4 km) long, with a further 300 yards (275 m) now filled in, and no locks. The Broadstone Branch was 0.75 miles (1.2 km) long with no locks and is now filled in. The Summit Level is 323.5 ft (98.6 m) O D Poolbeg. Note that the official numbering of the locks is from North Strand (No. 1) to the lock down from Richmond Harbour into the River Camlin (No. 46). L.T.C.Rolt in his book *Green & Silver* numbered the tidal lock into the River Liffey No. 1 and the North Strand lock No. 2 etc. which might cause readers some confusion.

The stretch of canal between Dublin and Mullingar is navigable. Small boats (not exceeding 6ft (1.83 m) beam and approximately 5ft (1.52 m) air draft) can pass through the culvert at Mullingar. Boats able to pass through the culvert and under the two low-level footbridges in Mullingar can travel on as far as the 38th Lock. Beyond Lock 38 the canal is in water as far as the 40th lock but the locks are not operational, and are unlikely to be so before 1998 at the earliest. Beyond the 40th lock the canal is currently being systematically dredged and rewatered. Between Abbeyshrule and Cloondara there are a further six culverted road crossings of the Main Line of the canal, and there are two culverted road crossings of the Longford Branch. In due course these will be replaced by new bridges but no dates can be given for the removal of these obstructions to navigation.

Speed

SPEED LIMIT:	4 mph; 6 km/h
LUAS TEORAINN:	4 mile san uair
	6 cilimeadar san uair
HÖCHSTGESCHWINDIGKEIT:	6 km/h
LIMITATION DE VITESSE:	6 km/h
LIMITE DI VELOCITÀ:	6 km all'ora

Permits Permits for lock passages and mooring must be obtained from the Waterways Service (see above). Charges: 50p per lock; £10 per month for mooring; £100 per annum for lock passage and mooring.

Dimensions The size of the smallest lock (No. 18) is:

length	75.0 ft (22.9 m)
breadth	13.3 ft (4.0 m)
depth on cill	4.7 ft (1.4 m)

The tidal lock into the River Liffey is 174.0 ft x 24.5 ft (53 m x 7.5m).
Headroom at the lowest bridge (railway bridge below 7th lock, Liffey Junction) is 10.0ft (3.05 m).

Equipment Boats must show a name or number, a valid permit from the Waterways Service and have sufficient crew to handle them effectively. A lock key is essential (see page 38). Be careful to observe the correct locking procedure and comply with Waterways Service bye-laws.

Traffic Keep to the right.

Lock Working (Uphill) The banks for some distance below many locks are extremely steep. As landing jetties are not provided jumping ashore in order to work the lock can be very hazardous. Thus it is advisable always to put a crew member ashore well before each lock is reached.

Moorings Do not tie up at locks or bridges so as to obstruct the navigation.

Water At time of going to press, the only canalside tap is located at the Confey Amenity Area (Map 2). Access to the tap can be made by contacting the Waterways Service in advance. From Spring 1997 drinking water will be available from a tap with hose fitting at Furey's public house, Moyvalley (Maps 5 and 6).

Diesel Fuel The only convenient source of marked diesel is at Kelly's garage, Kilcock (Map 4). The garage is on the opposite side of the R148 road from the canal, and thus the fuel would need to be carried across the road in cans. Opening hours: Monday-Friday 08.30 to 19.00; Saturday 09.00 to 17.30; closed Sunday and public holidays.

Safety Lock chambers are not equipped with ladders or lifebuoys. It is advisable to wear life jackets in canoes and small boats at all times, and when passing through locks in larger boats. Swimming is not allowed in any lock, harbour or dock.

Health The quality of water in the canal is generally good but, unlike tap water, it is untreated and micro-organisms are naturally present. The risk of contracting illness (including Weil's Disease) is small, but you should take sensible precautions:

- cover any cuts with a waterproof dressing;
- wash with clean water after canal activities;
- if you become ill within two weeks, let your doctor know that you have been in contact with untreated water.

Dry Docks There are dry docks at Mullingar Harbour and at Richmond Harbour, Cloondara. That at Mullingar will remain inaccessible to boats until the culvert at the site of Moran's Bridge is replaced by a navigable bridge. The dry dock at Richmond Harbour is accessible from the River Shannon via the 46th lock. Permission to use the dock is obtainable from the Waterways Service and the charge is £11 per day.

Slips There are slips at Confey (12th level between Collins Bridge and Cope Bridge, near Leixlip, map 2), at Maynooth Harbour (map 3), at Enfield Harbour (map 5), at Thomastown Harbour (map 7), at Mullingar Harbour (map 9), at Ballinea Harbour (map 10) and at Abbeyshrule Harbour (map 11).

Towpaths The towpath along the canal is now designated **"The Royal Canal Way"**. It is walkable from the 1st lock to the 40th lock and is being cleared further as restoration proceeds towards the Shannon and Longford. Signposts have been erected at each road bridge between Clonsilla and Mullingar and, eventually, signposting will be extended to cover the whole length of the canal.

Maps The maps in this guide are based on the Ordnance Survey (Permit No. 4179). The Royal Canal is covered by the half inch Ordnance Survey sheets 12, 13 & 16, and as they become available, the new 1:50,000 Discovery Series Sheets 40, 41, 48, 49 and 50.

Bus Services The information given is correct at the time of going to press. It should be noted that in remoter areas the services tend to be very infrequent, no more than one or two buses per day in each direction. Reference should be made to the Bus Eireann Local and Expressway Timetable for full information.

Further Reading

Ireland's Royal Canal 1789 - 1992, Ruth Delany, Lilliput Press, 1992.
The Royal Canal, Peter Clarke, Elo Publications, 1992.
Ireland's Inland Waterways, Ruth Delany, Appletree Press, 1986, reprinted 1993.
Green and Silver, L.T.C.Rolt, 3rd edition Athlone Branch IWAI 1993. Includes a description of a voyage along the Royal Canal in 1946.
Royal Canal Corridor Study: Spencer Dock-Kilcock, report prepared for Dept. of Arts, Culture & the Gaeltacht by RPS Cairns,1995.

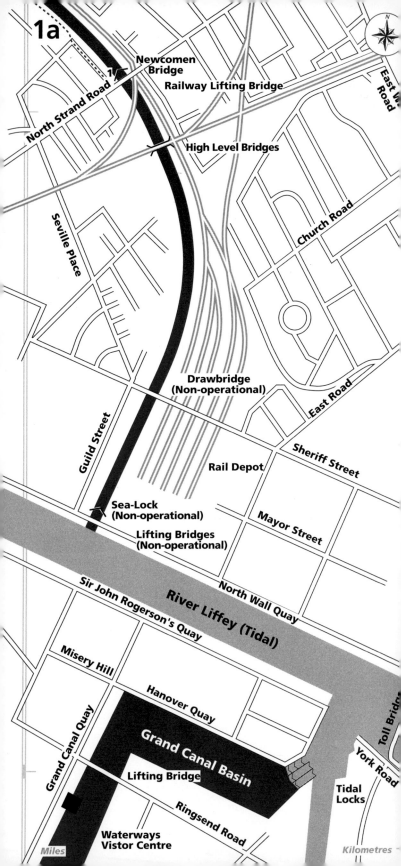

SPENCER DOCK (ENTRY TO ROYAL CANAL FROM RIVER LIFFEY AND GRAND CANAL)

The Royal Canal begins at **Spencer Dock** on the north bank of the tidal **River Liffey**. Prior to closure in 1961 the canal was connected with the river by a **sea lock**, the lower gates of which were situated under the innermost of the pair of **lifting bridges** on **North Wall Road**. **Spencer Dock** was formerly a wide stretch of waterway extending for over half a mile (approximately 1 km), and crossed by **Sheriff Street drawbridge** and three closely-spaced high level bridges carrying railway lines into Connolly Station. In the 1970s some of the dock area was in-filled and built over by CIE, considerably narrowing the canal between the **sea lock** and **Sheriff Street Bridge**.

At the inner end of **Spencer Dock**, just below **Newcomen Bridge**, the canal is also crossed by a single track **railway loop line at low level**. The original bridge was removed and the canal culverted through two 4 ft (1.22 m) diameter Armco pipes after closure of the canal in 1961. It is planned to install a new lifting bridge in 1997.

Neither the **sea lock**, the pair of **North Wall lifting bridges** nor **Sheriff Street drawbridge** are at present operational. Thus although **Spencer Dock** has been dredged, it will only be navigable at certain states of the tide, mainly due to the low headroom under bridges. For instance, boats will need to enter from the **River Liffey** around low water in order to clear the **North Wall Bridges,** and wait just north of the **sea lock** in a specially dredged **mooring area** for half tide. They must then proceed under **Sheriff Street Bridge** well before high water, entering the **1st lock** near high water. The exact timings are dependent upon tide height on any particular day, and the draft and air-draft of each vessel. Anyone contemplating this journey, either to or from the **River Liffey** or **Grand Canal Basin,** should first obtain an **Information Leaflet** from the Waterways Service. It will be available free of charge once navigation is restored.

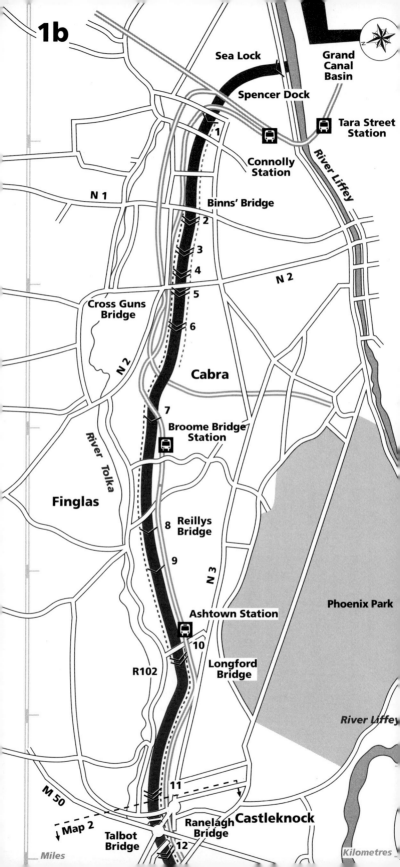

SPENCER DOCK, DUBLIN
TO 12TH LOCK, BLANCHARDSTOWN

Beyond the **first lock** the canal rises steeply out of the city through a succession of double locks passing Croke Park, Mountjoy Prison, the junction with the **Broadstone Branch** (now filled in) and Shandon Mills, Phibsborough. Just below the **7th lock**, at Liffey Junction, the railway line to the west crosses the canal to the south side, along which it is to be a constant companion all the way to Ballinea Bridge, west of Mullingar. From **Reilly's Bridge** the canal leaves the city behind and begins to assume a rural aspect which continues for almost the whole of its remaining 87 miles (140 km) to the River Shannon. There is a very attractive tree-lined stretch of waterway between the 10th and 11th locks, but it is soon followed by a new complex of bridges and an aqueduct associated with the junction of the M50 motorway and the Navan Road (N3).

History Work began on the Dublin sections of the Royal Canal in 1789 and continued through the 1790s with many delays caused by inaccurate surveys. The **Broadstone Branch** was not completed until 1801. **Foster Aqueduct**, a well-known city landmark on this branch, was demolished in 1951. There was a hotel at **Broadstone Harbour**, part of which became No. 1 Phibsborough Road. Drinking water was drawn from the harbour for the nearby City Basin until the 1860s. The Royal Canal Company reneged on its obligation to build docks at the junction with the River Liffey. Spencer Dock, which opened in 1873, was eventually constructed by the Midland Great Western Railway Company, which had bought the canal in 1845. **Broome Bridge**, like many of the bridges, is named after one of the early directors of the canal company but it is more notable for its connection with the Dublin-born mathematician and Astronomer Royal, Sir William Rowan Hamilton. A plaque on the bridge records that as he walked by on 16 October 1843, on his way from Dunsink Observatory, in a flash of genius he discovered the fundamental formula for quaternion multiplication, $i^2 = j^2 = k^2 = ijk = -1$.

Locks

1	tidal
2 (double)	21.6ft (6.60m) rise
3 (double)	17.7ft (5.40m) rise
4 (double)	17.6ft (5.35m) rise
5 (double)	18.0ft (5.50m) rise
6 (double)	17.4ft (5.30m) rise
7	8.5ft (2.60m) rise
8	8.8ft (2.70m) rise
9	6.9ft (2.10m) rise
10 (double)	18.0ft (5.50m) rise
11 (double)	18.2ft (5.55m) rise
12 (double)	18.4ft (5.60m) rise

Facilities

Pubs, shops: Binns' Bridge & Cross Guns Bridge.
Pub & restaurant: Talbot Bridge.
Railway Stations: Broome Bridge & Ashtown.
Bus Services: Ashtown (N3 road) 22B, 37, 38, 39, 39A, 70.
Talbot Bridge, Blanchardstown (Navan Road 500m) 38, 39, 39A, 70, 76A, 237.

BLANCHARDSTOWN TO LOUISA BRIDGE, NEAR LEIXLIP

Leaving **12th Lock, Blanchardstown**, the canal gradually enters a deep cutting through Carpenterstown quarry. For a distance of about 2 miles (3 km) to Clonsilla it passes through what is known as the **Deep Sinking**. At its deepest part the towpath is carried some 30 ft (9 m) above the water. Care should be taken when passing through this stretch as the channel width is very restricted. It is also a very pleasant walk along the towpath, but beware the steep drop to the canal. Beyond the cutting the canal passes between the stone piers of a bridge that once carried the Dublin & Meath Railway line to Navan, and then into more open country north of Lucan. There is a good road approach to the **boat slip** near **Leixlip** which gives access to this 7.5 mile (12 km) long level. Reasonable notice must be given to the Waterways Service to arrange for access to the Amenity Area and slip. About 1 mile (1.5 km) from the slip the canal bends sharply to the south and canal and railway are carried across the **Ryewater** by a massive earth embankment with the river flowing through a tunnel 100 ft (30 m) below. Between the **Ryewater Aqueduct** and **Louisa Bridge** and just to the west of the canal are the remains of **Leixlip Spa**, which was originally discovered by workmen building the embankment in the 1790s and became a fashionable watering place.

History This was a most controversial stretch of the canal because it became generally known that an unnecessary deviation to the south had been made to bring the canal through Maynooth at the request of the Duke of Leinster who was a prominent member of the company. A more northerly route would have avoided the **Deep Sinking** and the costly **Ryewater Aqueduct** but would have required an additional lock. The cutting, hewn and blasted through the hard black calcareous stone, cost more than £40,000, £10,000 of which was spent on tools and gunpowder. The aqueduct took six long years to construct and cost £27,000. The **Deep Sinking**, being so narrow, made the passing of canal boats impossible and the horses towing the boats were sometimes dragged into the canal. In November 1845 there was a serious accident in the cutting when the evening passenger boat to Longford from Dublin struck a stone on the side of the canal, heeled over and filled, drowning sixteen people.

The **7.5 mile (12 km) long level above the 12th Lock** was the first restoration project tackled by the newly formed Royal Canal Amenity Group in 1974.

Facilities

All Services: Lucan and Leixlip, some distance south of the canal.
Railway Stations: Castleknock, Coolmine, Leixlip Confey, Leixlip Louisa Bridge.
Bus Services: Granard Bridge 22B, 239, (Park Lodge, 150m) 37, 237. Kirkpatrick Bridge 237, (Carpenterstown Park, 250m) 37. Kennan Bridge (Clonsilla Road, 350m) 239. Callaghan Bridge 39A, 39X, 239. Cope Bridge 66A. Louisa Bridge 66.
Slip: Confey, Between Collins Bridge and Cope Bridge on north bank.
Water: Confey Amenity Area (access to tap by contacting Waterways Service).
Telephone: Cope Bridge (100m south of bridge).
Boat Hire: Royal Canal Cruisers, 12th Lock.

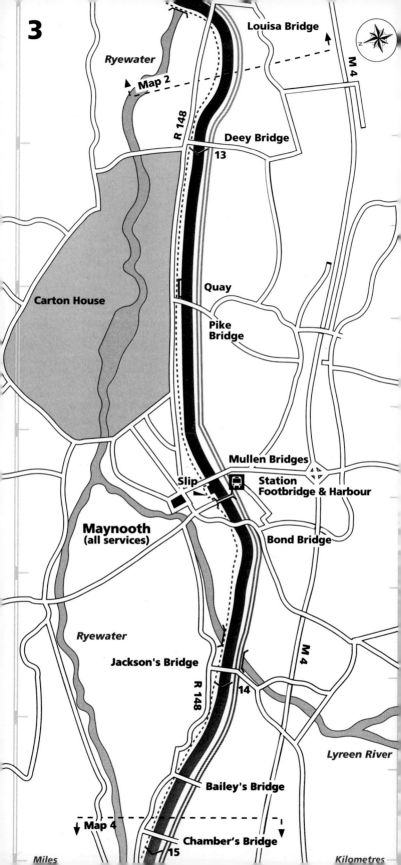

3

Ryewater

Louisa Bridge

M4

Map 2

R 148

Deey Bridge

13

Carton House

Quay

Pike Bridge

Mullen Bridges

Slip

Station Footbridge & Harbour

Maynooth (all services)

Bond Bridge

Ryewater

Jackson's Bridge

R 148

M4

14

Lyreen River

Bailey's Bridge

Map 4

Chamber's Bridge

15

Miles

Kilometres

LOUISA BRIDGE, NEAR LEIXLIP, TO CHAMBER'S BRIDGE, 15TH LOCK, NEAR KILCOCK

About a mile (1.5 km) from **Louisa Bridge**, **13th lock** marks the end of the 7.5 mile (12 km) level from Blanchardstown. The canal is closely hemmed in for the next few miles by the road on the north side and the ever-present railway on the south bank. The canal skirts the grounds of **Carton House**, formerly the seat of the Dukes of Leinster and there is a restored wharf just east of **Pike Bridge** which served the Estate. The **new Mullen Bridge** carrying the Straffan Road across the canal is an excellent example of the combination of modern engineering techniques and a design in complete sympathy with the 200 year old **Mullen Bridge** alongside. At **Maynooth** there is a fine harbour and **boat slip**. The canal follows the boundary wall of St. Patrick's College before climbing up through two single locks to the 15th level approaching **Kilcock**. **Jackson's Bridge** at **14th lock** is one of only two bridges on the canal with a separate arch for the towpath, the other being Newcomen Bridge over the tail of the 1st lock.

History   **13th Lock, Deey Bridge**, had the reputation among the old Royal Canal boatmen of being haunted and they would never moor there for the night. It was at **Carton House** that the Duke of Leinster lived who had insisted on the deviation of the canal. The original **Carton House** was remodelled by Richard Cassels in 1739/47 for the 19th Earl of Kildare in splendid style. After surmounting great difficulties the canal was eventually opened to **Kilcock** in 1796. **Maynooth Harbour**, although laid out at this time, was not actually completed until some years later.

St. Patrick's College, Maynooth was established in 1795 "for the better education of persons professing the Popish or Roman Catholic religion", to educate young men at home rather than force them to go to Europe. The buildings are two squares of courts built around the original Stoyte House and the architecture has been the subject of much criticism. At the gateway to the college is the keep and gatehouse of a Norman Fitzgerald castle, currently being restored by the National Monuments and Historic Properties Service of the Department of Arts, Culture and the Gaeltacht. The former Fitzgerald Chapel inside the grounds of the college is now the Church of Ireland church.

Locks

13	9.0ft (2.75m) rise
14	9.7ft (2.95m) rise
15	8.7ft (2.65m) rise

Facilities

All Services: Maynooth.
Railway Station: Maynooth.
Bus Services: Maynooth, 66, 66X, 67A, Provincial and Expressway services. Road adjoining canal, 66.
Slip: Maynooth Harbour, north bank opposite station.

4

To Maynooth

Chambers
Bridge

R 148

15

Map 3

M 4

Ryewater

Harbour
Shaws Bridge

16

Kilcock
(all sevices)

Allen or Spin
Bridge

R 407

McLoughlin Bridge

17 Fern's Lock

N 4

Long Level

Map 5

To Enfield

Miles

Kilometres

CHAMBER'S BRIDGE 15TH LOCK, THROUGH KILCOCK

4

Leaving **15th lock** the canal closes again with the road as it approaches **Kilcock**, where it opens out into a fine harbour. **Shaw's Bridge** and **16th lock (double)** are immediately above the harbour and then, skirting the town, which is almost hidden from view by trees, the canal passes through a most attractive stretch to **Allen Bridge**, known locally as **Spin Bridge**. From here is a stretch of 1.5 miles (2.5 km) to **17th lock, Fern's or Ferran's lock (double)**, the start of the 20-mile (32 km) Long Level to Thomastown. Immediately below **17th lock** an important feeder enters the canal drawn from the upper reaches of the **Ryewater** which accompanies the canal here for some distance.

From **17th lock** to **Cloncurry Bridge** is an attractive tree-lined stretch of waterway. Following restoration, the towpath is now located on the south bank.

History   With the canal completed to **Kilcock** and some boats in operation by 1796, the company had to seek further aid from parliament to continue the works. This aid was granted reluctantly in the form of a debenture loan of £25,000 because it was felt that this was the only way to safeguard the interests of the many small share holders who had invested in the company. The company in turn had to agree to complete the canal to the end of the Long Level at Thomastown without seeking further aid.

The stretch from **Fern's lock** to **Enfield** passes through Cappa bog and proved a laborious and expensive undertaking with problems caused by the sides slipping and the bottom swelling up so that by 1800 the company was once again in financial difficulty and the works were halted just beyond **Enfield**.

The Kilcock Branch of the RCAG was formed in 1982. Marvellous work was done in the ensuing months and in less than a year the appearance of the canal through **Kilcock** was transformed. Situated beside a main road **Kilcock Harbour** inevitably became the Group's showpiece. The opening of the new bypass restored some peace and calm to the town and added enormously to the amenity potential of the harbour area.

Locks

16 (double)	16.2ft (4.95m) rise
17 (double)	16.5ft (5.05m) rise

Facilities

All Services: Kilcock.
Bus Services: Kilcock, 66, Provincial and Expressway services. Road adjoining canal, 66.

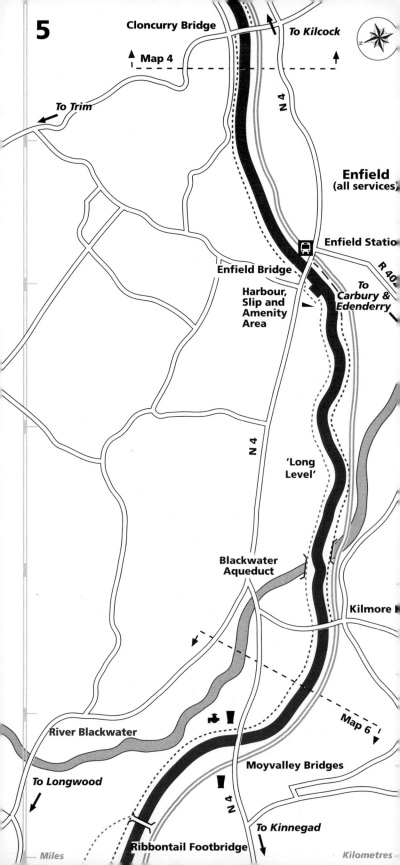

5

Cloncurry Bridge

To Kilcock

↑ Map 4

To Trim

N 4

Enfield (all services)

Enfield Station

R 40

Enfield Bridge

To Carbury & Edenderry

Harbour, Slip and Amenity Area

N 4

'Long Level'

Blackwater Aqueduct

Kilmore

Map 6

River Blackwater

Moyvalley Bridges

To Longwood

N 4

To Kinnegad

Miles

Ribbontail Footbridge

Kilometres

CLONCURRY BRIDGE THROUGH ENFIELD TO MOYVALLEY

From **Cloncurry Bridge** the tarred road follows the canal for about a mile (1.5 km) before swinging away. Soon the canal enters a deep tree-shaded cutting and passes under the N 4 road as it enters **Enfield**. The restored **harbour** is situated on the north bank within the newly created **Amenity Park**, through which there is access to the **slipway**. The towpath on the south bank is also surfaced for about a mile (1.5 km) with a turning place for cars where it ends. This is a part of the canal much favoured by anglers and frequently used for fishing competitions. Two and a quarter miles (3.5 km) beyond Enfield the canal crosses the **River Blackwater Aqueduct** before reaching **Kilmore Bridge**. The tree-lined stretch from here to **Moyvalley** is one of the most attractive on the whole canal.

History   From **Cloncurry Bridge** to **Enfield** the engineers were faced with a difficult section of deep sinking in order to keep the canal on the same level to avoid lockage. When the water was eventually admitted, the banks, which were made of fine sand, tended to slip into the canal.

The restoration of **Enfield Harbour**, the construction of the **boat slip** and the development of the **park** were all undertaken jointly by the Enfield Community Council and the Enfield Branch of the RCAG, mainly by way of a sponsored Community Youth Training Project and a Social Employment Scheme.

In 1991 the Waterways Service employed a specialist contractor to repair the **Blackwater Aqueduct**, the spreading and leaking north side of which had been stabilised by enormous timber props for longer than anyone can recall. Restoration involved grouting and tie-rodding. The fault was diagnosed as inferior construction methods, which is surprising in view of the excellent masonry work elsewhere on the canal.

There was once a fine canal hotel at **Moyvalley** but the ruins were demolished in 1977 to make way for the approach road for the new bridge. The hotel opened to travellers in 1807 and in the years that followed it was reported to be "the best of its kind and the best kept of any in Ireland". Then business began to decline and the canal company sought a tenant but he did not fare much better. In the 1820s when the Ribbonmen were active in the area and were carrying out attacks on the boats, a local police force was raised and stationed here. Another attempt to operate a hotel failed in the 1830s and, eventually, the building was purchased by Mr. Switzer who set up a Hydropathy establishment and built a Bath House. This proved a successful venture for some years but, eventually, Mr. Switzer decided to close down, although he continued to live in the house until his death in 1891. Thereafter, there were a number of owners until Mr. Mulvaney vacated the house in the 1930s and it gradually became ruinous.

Facilities

All Services: Enfield.
Pub with public telephone: Moyvalley.
Restaurant: Moyvalley.
Railway Station: Enfield.
Bus Services: Enfield, Provincial and Expressway service. Moyvalley, Provincial service.
Slip: Enfield Harbour, north bank.

6

To Enfield ↑

Moyvalley
Bridges

River Blackwater

↑ Map 5

Ribbontail
Footbridge

Longwood

Long Level

Harbour

Boyne Aqueduct

Longwood Road
Aqueduct

River Boyne

Blackshade Bridge

N 4

R 161

Killyon Bridge

Hill of Down

Map 7 ▼

R 161

Miles

Ballasport Bridge

Kilometres

MOYVALLEY TO BALLASPORT BRIDGE

This is a fine stretch of waterway. The canal crosses the **Longwood Road Aqueduct** and the impressive three-arched aqueduct over the **River Boyne**, with the railway viaduct nearby. From Hill of Down the canal is through more open country with typical hedgerows.

History In 1801 the canal company asked the newly elected Directors General of Inland Navigation for financial aid and they sent their engineer, John Brownrigg, to inspect the works. At this time the canal ended at the aqueduct over the **Blackwater** but the line was laid out across the **Boyne** and on towards **Kinnegad**. He said that the line was "as bad and as expensive as can be imagined" and the directors of the canal company were persuaded to alter the line to the north, away from **Kinnegad**. Some of the line had actually been excavated and it is possible to trace parts of the abandoned canal and to see the point at which it diverged from the present line about halfway between **Blackshade Bridge** and **Hill of Down**. A grant of £95,856 was given to the company with a proviso that the canal must be completed to Mullingar without further aid and that docks should be constructed at the junction with the River Liffey in Dublin.

The **Ribbontail footbridge** was erected to facilitate people going to the nearby church but it is not clear how it received its name. There is possibly a connection with the Ribbonmen who are said to have congregated around the bridge when they were active in the area. The bridge was restored by the Longwood Branch of the RCAG.

A major breach of the embankment, east of the Longwood Road Aqueduct, occurred in June, 1993. Its repair over the following months by the Waterways Service was the biggest restoration project on the canal in any single location.

When the canal was in commercial use, the harbour beside the Longwood Road Aqueduct was known locally as "Boyne Dock".

Facilities

Shops, pubs, telephone, garage: Longwood (about 1 mile (1.5 km); either along the boreen from Ribbontail Bridge or from the harbour beside Longwood Road Aqueduct).
Shop, Pub and Telephone: Hill of Down.
Bus Service: Longwood (very limited).

7

Ballasport
Bridge

Map 6

To Kinnegad

Long Level

Hyde
Park

Riverstown River

D'Arcy's Bridge

Harbour
& Slip

Thomastown Bridge

18

19

To Ballivor

20

R 156

Map 8

21

Killucan

To Cloghan

Riverstown Bridge

22

23

24

To Milltownpass

Miles

Kilometres

BALLASPORT BRIDGE TO RIVERSTOWN BRIDGE

At **Hill of Down** the railway line heads straight across a bog but the canal takes a more tortuous route. This can be a bleak and exposed section of canal until the wooded demesne of **Hyde Park** is reached near **D'Arcy's Bridge**. At **Thomastown** the canal widens out into a fine harbour fed by the Riverstown Supply before commencing the steep climb up to the summit level through a series of eight locks, spaced out at approximately 0.25 mile (0.5 km) intervals. From **Thomastown** to **Riverstown Bridge** there are now towpaths on both banks; that on the south side being driveable.

History   Having abandoned the line through Kinnegad, work continued on the new line to **Thomastown** and the canal was opened to here in 1805. One year earlier the rival canal, the Grand Canal, had been opened right through to the River Shannon. The old canal boats lying above **D'Arcy's Bridge** belong to the Leech Family of **Killucan**, who were the last bye-traders working on the canal before it closed. Some of the family still live in the area.

When, in 1985, the harbour at **Thomastown** was restored by the Killucan Branch of the RCAG, a new **boat slip** was constructed on the south bank. The eight locks of the **Killucan flight** were re-opened in 1989.

Locks

18	9.4ft (2.85m) rise
19	9.1ft (2.75m) rise
20	9.2ft (2.80m) rise
21	8.9ft (2.70m) rise

Facilities

Shop and Pub: Thomastown Harbour.
Shop, pub, telephone, garage: Killucan (about 1.5 miles (2.5 km) from Thomastown Bridge); Riverstown Bridge.
Slip: Thomastown Harbour, access beside pub on south bank.

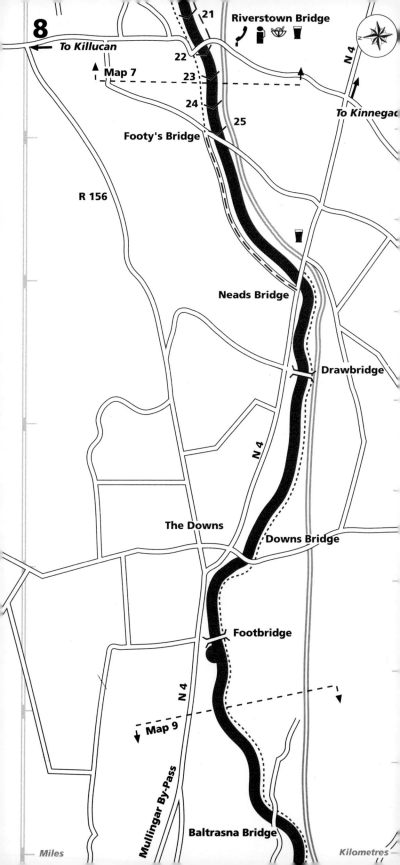

8

To Killucan

Map 7

R 156

Footy's Bridge

21
22
23
24
25

Riverstown Bridge

N 4

To Kinnegad

Neads Bridge

Drawbridge

N 4

The Downs

Downs Bridge

Footbridge

N 4

Map 9

Mullingar By-Pass

Baltrasna Bridge

Miles

Kilometres

RIVERSTOWN BRIDGE TO BALTRASNA BRIDGE

Continuing up the staircase there is a towpath on the north bank only from **Riverstown Bridge** and the railway rejoins the canal. This is a very attractive stretch. The **25th lock** marks the start of the 15-mile (24 km) **Summit level** (323.5 ft (98.6 m) OD Poolbeg), and at **Nead's Bridge** the canal once again passes under the N 4 road. Half a mile (nearly 1 km) beyond **Nead's Bridge** is a **lifting bridge** giving access to a farm on the south bank. This bridge has to be operated by boaters and should always be left in the lowered position. Road, rail and canal continue close together as far as **Downs Bridge** but from here the railway follows a more southerly route into **Mullingar** whilst the canal twists its way between road and rail. For about 1 mile (1.5 km) either side of **Baltrasna Bridge** the canal passes through a rock cutting reminiscent of the "Deep Sinking" through Carpenterstown but not as steep.

History   Beside the towpath, just above **23rd lock**, is one of the few remaining milestones to be found along the banks of the canal. It indicates 43 miles from here to Broadstone Harbour in statute miles, unlike the Grand Canal which has quite a number of mile stones marking the distance in statute miles on one bank and in Irish miles on the other.

Once again the engineers seem to have chosen a very difficult line for the canal approaching **Mullingar**. To preserve the level it was necessary to carve out a line for the canal through rock which proved very costly. The **Summit Level** as far as **Mullingar** was eventually opened to traffic in 1806 but the government grant had been long since exhausted and the company was once again facing financial difficulties.

The MGWRCo, which had acquired the Royal Canal with a view to building the railway line along its route, completed its railway line to Mullingar in 1848. Although the railway company's administration of the canal was subject to a government Board of Control, the canal inevitably did not prosper under railway management and its condition was allowed to deteriorate over the years.

The new road bridge, replacing **Nead's Bridge**, was finished in 1975. The original plans did not allow full navigational clearance but, following representations from the IWAI, the Minister for Local Government at the time, Mr. Tully, intervened and Westmeath County Council agreed to his request to alter the plans. This was a turning point in the campaign for the restoration of the canal and, thereafter, permission for non-navigable bridges over the canal was refused.

Locks

22	8.5ft (2.60m) rise
23	8.7ft (2.65m) rise
24	8.7ft (2.65m) rise
25	8.5ft (2.60m) rise

Facilities

Shop, pub, telephone, garage: Riverstown Bridge.
Pub: Nead's Bridge.
Bus Service: Killucan (1.5 miles (2.5 km) north of Riverstown Bridge).

9

To Kinnegad

Baltrasna Bridge

By-Pass

To Kells

N4

N 52

Map 16

Culvert & Site of Morans Bridge

Lough Owel Feeder

Harbour

Saunders Bridge

To Rochfortbridge

Scanlan's Bridge

Green Bridge

Mullingar (all services)

N 52

Slip

Footbridge

To Edgeworthstown

New Bridge
(Under Construction)

Footbridge

To Ballynacargy

R392

Kilpatrick Bridge

To Ballymahon

Harbour & Slip

Belmont Bridge

Ballinea Bridges

Miles

Kilometres

BALTRASNA BRIDGE THROUGH MULLINGAR TO BALLINEA BRIDGE

Midway between **Baltrasna Bridge** and **Saunder's Bridge** a **feeder** enters from the south through twin stone culverts, known locally as the **"Pig's Nostril"**. There is a tendency for a silt bar to form in the channel, requiring regular dredging to maintain a navigable depth.

In the 1960s, **Moran's Bridge** on Austin Friars Street (Dublin road) was demolished and the culvert that replaced it now marks the head of navigation for boats exceeding 6 ft (1.8 m) beam and approximately 5 ft (1.5 m) air draft. The **harbour** at **Piper's Boreen** on the south bank of the canal, 350 yards (320 m) north of **Saunder's Bridge**, is a convenient turning and mooring point, being away from the busy road junction beside the culvert. A new bridge is to be built to replace the culvert.

The canal continues in a great loop to the north of the town before leaving to the south-west. Halfway around this loop, and just before the **main harbour**, the supply **feeder** enters from **Lough Owel**, two miles (3 km) to the north. Once navigable by dinghy, the combination of low level pipes across the channel and a concrete dam at the fish farm 1.25 miles (2 km) upstream from the harbour make this journey no longer possible (Map 16).

The extensive **harbour** at **Mullingar** is divided in two by **Scanlan's Bridge.** There is also a **dry dock** opening off the harbour (east side) and a **boat slip** west of the bridge. Leaving town the canal meets up with the railway again but at **Ballinea Bridge** they finally part company as the railway line turns south for Athlone. There is another **boat slip** into this level at **Ballinea Harbour** (north bank).

History Once again there was controversy about the line the canal should take at **Mullingar**. The original line was marked out and valued to run south of the town but this route involved a high embankment and so the northerly route was adopted following the contour of the land. The unique quality of **Lough Owel** water, because of its small catchment area, has made others turn envious eyes towards it and Westmeath County Council use it to supplement the town water supply. There is also a fish farm drawing water from the feeder. The water entering the feeder is controlled at a sluice-house at the point where the feeder leaves the lake.

Restoration

The **summit level** west of **Mullingar** is being dredged in stages. It is intended to complete the dredging of this level by the middle of 1998. It is a most attractive stretch of canal with a wide diversity of flora and fauna, to be enjoyed by walker and boater alike.

Facilities

All Services: Mullingar.
Railway Station: Mullingar.
Bus Services: Mullingar, Provincial and Expressway services.
Shop & telephone: Ballinea Bridge (about 0.25 mile (0.5 km) to the south).
Slips: Mullingar Harbour, north bank, west of Scanlan's Bridge. Ballinea Harbour, north bank.
Dry Dock: Mullingar Harbour (inaccessible at present).

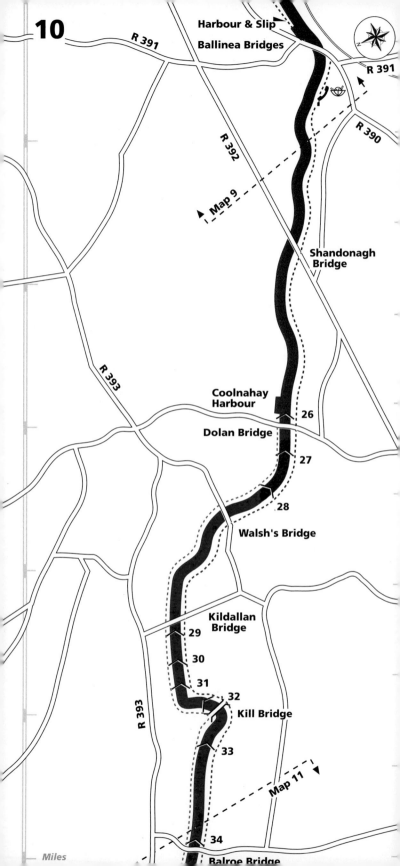

BALLINEA BRIDGE TO 34TH LOCK NEAR BALLYNACARGY

This is a very attractive section of the canal. The descent from **Coolnahay** towards the Shannon is rather more gradual than the climb up to the summit from Thomastown, the first ten locks being spaced out over the 5 miles (8 km) to **Ballynacargy**. From **Coolnahay** the canal twists its way towards the **Inny** valley seeking to avoid high ground. By doing so it also avoids most forms of habitation other than the occasional house or farm. Thus once **Ballinea** is left behind there are no facilities along this stretch of waterway.

History At **Ballinea** there is an interesting example of a "skew bridge", of which there are only two on the Royal Canal, the other being Ballasport Bridge, which is only very slightly skewed. There are engineering difficulties about designing the courses of skew humpbacked bridges and the Romans were probably the first to overcome these problems. Early canal engineers usually took the easy way out and realigned the roads to cross the canal at right angles.

The canal was completed to **Coolnahay** by 1809 but by this time the company was heavily in debt and the small surplus revenue coming in from the part of the canal that was operational was insufficient to pay the interest on the debt let alone continue work on the canal. In addition, controversy had arisen with the Grand Canal Company about the line the canal was to follow to the Shannon. Any deviation from the line actually authorised by parliament, which threatened the trade on the Grand Canal, was strongly resisted by this company. Finally, the government was asked to intervene in the dispute and this led to a decision to inquire into the financial affairs of both companies. It became obvious that the Royal Canal Company was no longer in a position to complete the canal and so it was decided that the company should be dissolved and the canal completed using public funds. The government felt that it would be an even greater loss to the country to leave the canal in an unfinished state after so much public and private money had been invested in the scheme. In 1813 the Directors General of Inland Navigation took over control of the concern with instructions to complete the canal to the Shannon.

Restoration

Restoration as far as **Ballynacargy** was completed in 1996. However full access to this stretch awaits the construction of a new bridge in **Mullingar** to replace the culvert at the Dublin Road. Restoration westwards from **35th Lock** is ongoing. Apart from a short stretch of the summit level, dredging of the Main Line will be completed in 1997 and the refurbishment of locks will continue, together with extensive repairs to the banks and bed of the canal.

Locks

26	7.2ft (2.20m) fall
27	7.0ft (2.15m) fall
28	8.0ft (2.45m) fall
29	9.5ft (2.90m) fall
30	9.0ft (2.75m) fall
31	8.8ft (2.70m) fall
32	9.0ft (2.75m) fall
33	9.6ft (2.95m) fall
34	9.4ft (2.85m) fall

Facilities

Slip: Ballinea Harbour, north bank.

11

Balroe Bridge 34

Map 10

Ballynacargy

35 Harbour

Ballynacargy Bridge

36

Accommodation Bridge

Kiddy's Bridge

37

Accommodation Bridge

R 393

38

Kelly's Bridge

Ledwith's Bridge

River Blackwater

Ballymaglavy Bog

River Inny

Bog Bridge

R 393

Quinns Bridge

Airfield

Aqueduct

Abbeyshrule

Map 12

Scally's Bridge

Webb's Bridge and Culvert

Harbour

Miles

Slip

Kilometres

34TH LOCK NEAR BALLYNACARGY TO RIVER INNY AQUEDUCT AND ABBEYSHRULE

Ballynacargy owes its existence largely to the canal and was an important trading centre. Leaving here there are three more locks before the canal enters **Ballymaglavy Bog**. It is a pleasant but exposed journey across the bog. After traversing the bog the canal enters County Longford, and crosses the **River Inny** by an imposing **aqueduct** which was underpinned several years ago when the Inny drainage scheme was being carried out. **Abbeyshrule Airfield** is located beside the canal on the north bank just before the canal crosses the river and access to the airfield is along the towpath. After crossing the **Inny** the canal turns sharply to the south and follows the river valley into **Abbeyshrule**.

History   Faced with the daunting task of completing the canal, the Directors General of Inland Navigation entered into a contract with an engineering firm, Henry, Mullins & McMahon, to carry out the entire extension to the Shannon for £145,000. The plaque on the **Whitworth Aqueduct** over the Inny is difficult to decipher. It reads:

"This Aqueduct with the entire Royal Canal Extension 24.5 miles in length, having 21 Locks, 38 Bridges and 40 Tunnels, with several extensive Harbours, Quays and other Works of Masonry was designed by John Killaly Esq., Engineer to the Directors General of Inland Navigation and executed under their Direction in the short space of 3 years by the Undertakers, Henry, Mullins & McMahon." (The mileage is in Irish Miles - 2240 yards)

At **Abbeyshrule**, as its name denotes, the remains of a Cistercian Abbey are to be found: follow the signpost through the graveyard and through two further gates. The place was colonised from Mellifont around 1150 but the earliest buildings date from around 1200. The oldest buildings are the chancel, altered in the sixteenth century to form a chapel, and the tower, which was later blocked by a wall with three compartments. The other tower was built in post-Reformation times. There is an interesting shaft of a High Cross in the graveyard which has a strange horseshoe device on it.

Restoration

Rewatering the section through **Ballymaglavy Bog** presents great problems. After closure in 1961 a serious breach occurred in the bed of the canal halfway across the bog. Staunching the breach was a major task tackled by the local branch of the RCAG in 1982. The banks had also subsided and had to be raised. This allowed the level to be rewatered but unfortunately another breach occurred close by in 1990. A temporary repair was effected by the OPW in 1992 and permanent repairs will be carried out in due course. Owing to the poor condition of the canal banks through the bog the level, at present, is only partially filled. The depth is approximately 3.5 ft (1 m).

Locks

35	9.0ft (2.75m) fall
36	9.8ft (3.00m) fall
37	9.1ft (2.75m) fall
38	9.2ft (2.80m) fall

Facilities

Shops, pubs, telephone, garage: Ballynacargy.
Bus Service: Ballynacargy (Wed. & Sat. only).
Shop, pub, restaurant: Abbeyshrule.
Slip: Abbeyshrule Harbour, north bank.

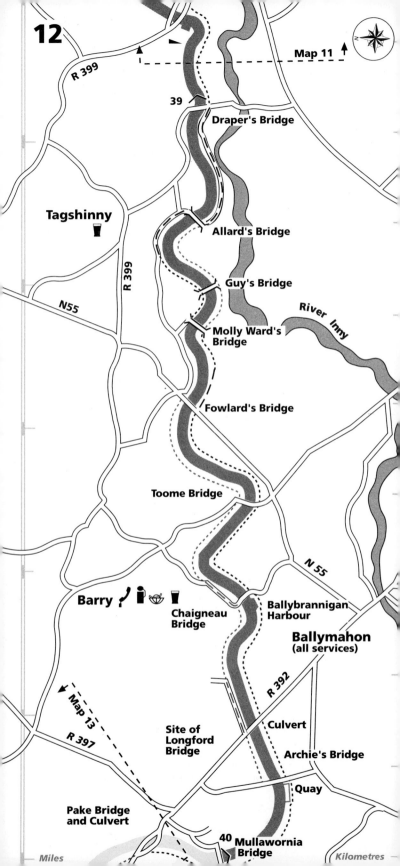

12

R 399

Map 11 ↑

39

Draper's Bridge

Tagshinny

R 399

N55

Allard's Bridge

Guy's Bridge

River Inny

Molly Ward's
Bridge

Fowlard's Bridge

Toome Bridge

N 55

Barry

Chaigneau
Bridge

Ballybrannigan
Harbour

Ballymahon
(all services)

R 392

Map 13

R 397

Site of
Longford
Bridge

Culvert

Archie's Bridge

Quay

**Pake Bridge
and Culvert**

40 **Mullawornia
Bridge**

Miles   _Kilometres_

ABBEYSHRULE TO PAKE BRIDGE NEAR BALLYMAHON

The level from **39th lock** is the longest on the western end of the canal, extending for 7 miles (11 km). The canal follows the contours of the Inny valley and this is undoubtedly the most tortuous section of the whole line. As far as **Archie's Bridge** there are now towpaths on both banks. For the first 4 miles (6.5 km) the canal is narrow and enclosed with high hedgerows so that the nearby river is only visible occasionally.

Passing under **Chaigneau Bridge**, known locally as Brannigan Bridge, the canal opens out into **Ballybrannigan Harbour** where there is a quay and store and the remains of another ruined building which was the bell-house and waiting room for passengers. This stretch of canal around **Ballymahon** is through more open country and parts of the canal are embanked. At the Ballymahon to Lanesborough Road the canal is culverted and **Longford Bridge** has been demolished. At **Archie's Bridge** there is a quay and the remains of two large stores. From here the canal curves around **Mullawornia Hill** following the contours. At this point the canal is only about 2 miles (3 km) from the River Shannon at Lough Ree but, instead of continuing west in the Inny valley, it takes a sharp turn to the north. Emerging from a cutting the canal enters **40th lock**, **Mullawornia**, and is carried along a rocky escarpment with the rock rising sheer above the east bank and falling away almost vertically on the opposite side. An extensive stone quarrying operation has eaten away a large portion of **Mullawornia Hill**. As can be imagined, there are excellent views towards Lough Ree.

History   Although the harbour and passage boat station were at **Ballybrannigan Harbour**, **Toome Bridge** was the place where passengers alighted to connect with Bianconi's cars to Athlone. There were quite a number of places along the route of the canal where coaching establishments provided connecting services. In the 1830s over 40,000 passengers were carried per year on the canal and the tonnage of goods rose to a peak of 100,000 tons per annum in the 1840s.

Restoration

The **40th level** was partially rewatered in 1993, and the **41st level** more recently. Both levels have required extensive bank repairs and this work is still in progress. Although no plans have yet been made to replace the several culverts in County Longford, the work should be undertaken by 1999.

The Ballymahon Branch of the RCAG was responsible for the preliminary clearance work undertaken in the area prior to the arrival of the dredgers in 1992. Ballybrannigan Harbour and all bridges were cleared of ivy and other growth and a considerable amount of towpath and channel clearance was done by way of a sponsored Social Employment Scheme.

Locks

39	9.8ft (3.00m) fall
40	10.1ft (3.10m) fall

Facilities

Pub: Tagshinny, (about 1 mile (1.5 km) from Draper's or Allard's Bridge).
All Services: Ballymahon (about 1 mile (1.5 km) from Toome Bridge, Ballybrannigan Harbour or culvert at site of Longford Bridge).
Shop, pub, telephone, petrol: Barry (about 1.5 miles (2.5 km) from Toome Bridge or Ballybrannigan Harbour).
Bus Service: Ballymahon, Provincial and Expressway services.

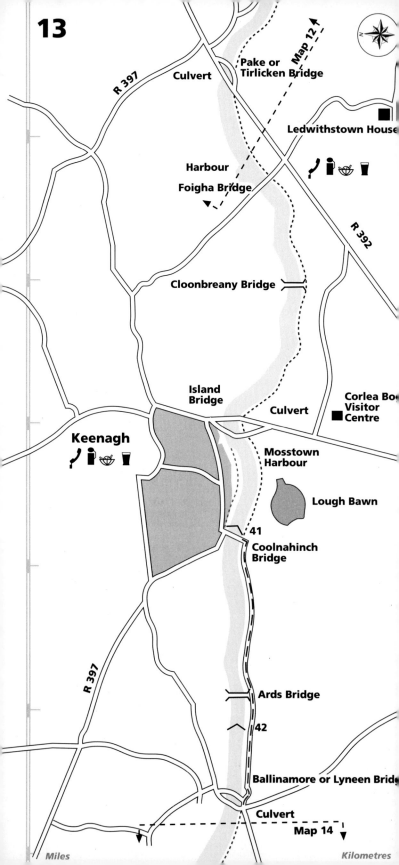

13

R 397

Culvert

Pake or
Tirlicken Bridge

Map 12

Ledwithstown House

R 392

Harbour
Foigha Bridge

Cloonbreany Bridge

Island
Bridge

Corlea Bog
Visitor
Centre

Culvert

Keenagh

Mosstown
Harbour

Lough Bawn

41
Coolnahinch
Bridge

R 397

Ards Bridge

42

Ballinamore or Lyneen Bridge

Culvert

Map 14

Miles

Kilometres

PAKE BRIDGE TO LYNEEN BRIDGE

Re-crossing the Ballymahon to Lanesborough road the canal is again culverted at **Pake Bridge**, although the original bridge is still standing alongside the realigned road. The canal continues in a northerly direction via **Foigha Harbour** to **Cloonbreany Bridge**, beyond which it widens out considerably as it passes across a windswept expanse of bog before reaching yet another culvert beside **Island Bridge**, and **Mosstown Harbour**. Beyond the harbour, which is within easy walking distance of **Keenagh** village, the canal enters a shallow cutting alongside the dense woodland of **Mosstown Estate** which continues as far as **Coolnahinch Lock**. From here to **Lyneen Bridge**, where there is another culvert, the canal is accompanied by a road which has superseded the towpath on the west bank.

History The Grand Canal Company opposed any suggestion that the Royal Canal should terminate in Lough Ree, a little over 2 miles (3 km) from **Mullawornia**, and the Government agreed that the purpose of the canal was to serve the north Shannon and, in particular, to provide a route for Lough Allen coal. Moreover, it was thought to be impractical to terminate the canal in a large lake where adverse weather conditions could hold up traffic for long periods. Thus the canal continues for another 12 miles (19 km) to the junction with the Shannon.

One mile (1.5 km) south of **Foigha Bridge** is **Ledwithstown House**, a very interesting small Georgian house built in 1746, the design of which is attributed to Richard Cassels. Originally the seat of the Ledwith family, the estate at one time covered some 2,000 acres. The last of the family to live there, William Ledwith, left in 1891. In 1911 the property was bought by Laurence Feeney, grandfather of the present owner. The house is at present being painstakingly restored and is open to visitors by appointment.

Between the canal and the Shannon lies a vast tract of bog over which, from as far back as 3,500 BC, a large network of wooden tracks was laid. When, in the 1960s, Bord na Mona brought its industry to **Corlea Bog** these trackways began to be uncovered. A preserved portion of the trackways and numerous important artefacts are on display in the **Corlea Bog Visitor Centre** about 1 mile (1.5 km) west of **Island Bridge.**

Mosstown House, the home of the Kingston family, was demolished in 1962 but visitors to **Keenagh** village can admire the clock tower (1875) with its clock still in working order. The entrance to the estate through a mile-long avenue of lime trees planted in 1850; the eagle-topped piers at the White Gate, built by Belgian refugees after the first World War; and the restored Pigeon House, the only one of its kind in the country, are also of interest.

Locks

41	10.0ft (3.05m) fall
42	10.1ft (3.10m) fall

Facilities

Shops, pubs, telephone, garage: Foigha Cross Roads, R392 (about 0.2 mile (0.3 km) south of Foigha Bridge).
Shops, pubs, telephone, garage: Keenagh (about 0.75 mile (1.2 km) from Island Bridge).
Bus Service: Keenagh (Saturdays only).
Ledwithstown House (see above): Open to visitors by appointment. Tel: 0902-32382.

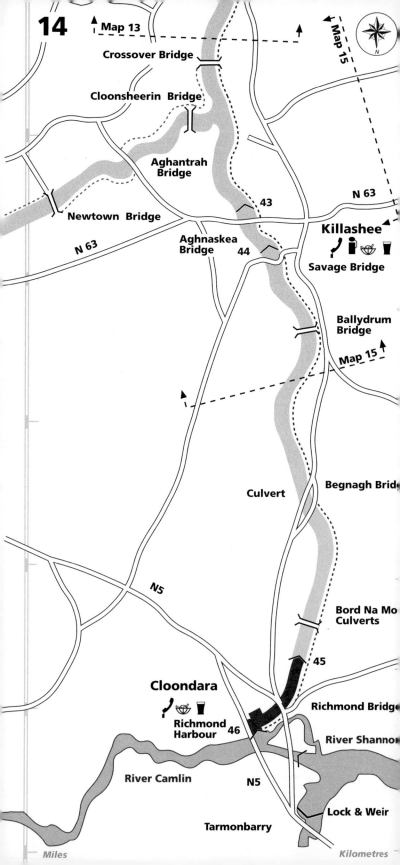

14

Map 13

Crossover Bridge

Cloonsheerin Bridge

Map 15

Aghantrah Bridge

43

N 63

Newtown Bridge

Killashee

N 63

Aghnaskea Bridge

44

Savage Bridge

Ballydrum Bridge

Map 15

Culvert

Begnagh Bridge

N 5

Bord Na Mo Culverts

45

Cloondara

Richmond Bridge

Richmond Harbour 46

River Shannon

River Camlin

N 5

Lock & Weir

Tarmonbarry

Miles

Kilometres

LOWER LYNEEN OR CROSSOVER BRIDGE TO RICHMOND HARBOUR, CLOONDARA, JUNCTION WITH THE RIVER SHANNON

The towpath along this section was very overgrown prior to restoration. The canal itself is hemmed in by dense hedgerows as far as **Crossover Bridge**, beyond which it enters more open country as it approaches the junction with the **Longford Branch** and continues on to the **43rd lock**, near **Killashee** village. About 250 yards (230 m) below this lock the bed of the canal suddenly becomes completely dry and remains so as far as the **44th lock**. There is obviously a swallow hole in the bottom of the canal through which all water disappears underground. Beside **Begnagh Bridge** is the last of the culverted road crossings on the main line, but before reaching the **45th lock** there are two culverts constructed by Bord na Mona, one a light-railway crossing, the other for machinery.

The last stretch of canal, from **Rinnmount** to **Cloondara**, was rewatered in 1972 by Shannon Navigation Division of The Office of Public Works. Access to **Richmond Harbour** from the Shannon is via the Camlin River from Lough Forbes or through the old Shannon Navigation lock and up a short length of canal from below Tarmonbarry. Water is pumped up from the Camlin to supply the harbour. The **dry dock** off the harbour has also been restored and can be availed of by arrangement with the Waterways Service.

History The canal was completed to **Richmond Harbour** in 1817 and in the following year the whole concern was handed over to the newly constituted New Royal Canal Company with a government appointed Board of Control to keep an eye on its affairs. However, the expected trade from the north Shannon did not materialise even after the completion of the Lough Allen Canal in 1821. The total cost of the canal from Dublin had been about £1.5 million and it had taken nearly thirty years to complete.

In the 1830s the distillery at **Cloondara** was producing some 70,000 gallons of whiskey a year and employing about 70 people; it subsequently became a cornmill and now processes animal hides. There are some interesting graveslabs in the graveyard beside the church in **Cloondara**. This was the site of an early monastery and hospice.

Restoration

Rewatering the short level between the **43rd and 44th locks** will obviously present problems as the bed of the canal will need to be sealed.

Locks

43	10.0ft (3.05m) fall
44	10.3ft (3.15m) fall
45	8.9ft (2.70m) fall
46	8.5ft (2.60m) fall

Facilities

Shops, pubs, telephone, garage: Killashee (west of the canal from 43rd or 44th lock).
Shop, pubs, telephone: Richmond Harbour, Cloondara.
Bus Service: Killashee. Tarmonbarry, N5 road (1 mile (1.5 km) north of Richmond Harbour) Provincial and Expressway services.
Dry Dock: Richmond Harbour (see page 2).

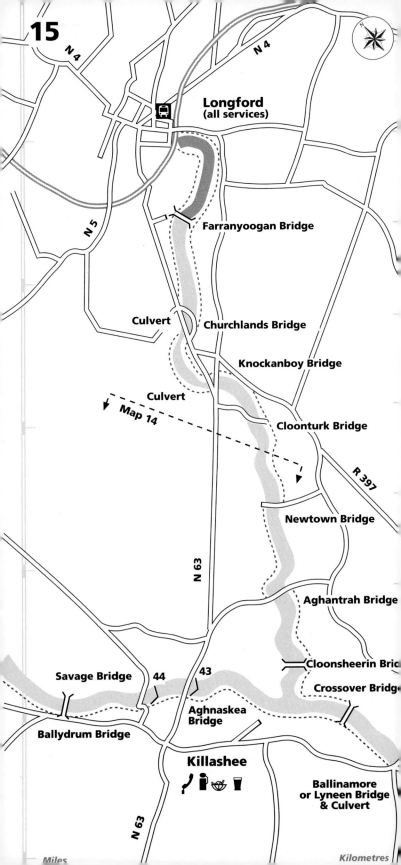

N 4

N 4

Longford
(all services)

N 5

Farranyoogan Bridge

Culvert

Churchlands Bridge

Knockanboy Bridge

Culvert

Map 14

Cloonturk Bridge

R 397

Newtown Bridge

N 63

Aghantrah Bridge

Cloonsheerin Bric

Savage Bridge

44

43

Crossover Bridge

Ballydrum Bridge

Aghnaskea
Bridge

Killashee

Ballinamore
or Lyneen Bridge
& Culvert

N 63

Miles

Kilometres

THE LONGFORD BRANCH

The **Longford Branch** is dry except for the section between **Farranyoogan Bridge** and **Longford**. The towpath is very overgrown in places but clearance is in progress. There are two culverted road crossings at **Knockanboy Bridge** and **Churchlands Bridge**. It is an attractive walk, much of it tree-lined. The final part of the canal where it passed under the railway and opened out into a harbour has been filled in and the branch now terminates south of the railway. The last mile (1.5 km) was dredged in 1992 and rewatered by placing stop planks under **Farranyoogan Bridge**, so that it can be developed as an amenity for the town. A supply of water is assured because the upper part of the branch is fed by springs.

History **Lower Lyneen** or **Crossover Bridge**, as its name denotes, was built at the same time as the **Longford Branch** in the 1820s to enable the towing horses to be brought across to the other bank to gain access to the branch towpath.

With the canal completed to **Cloondara** in 1817 and all debts wiped out, the company stood a chance of success and the next 25 years were to prove reasonably prosperous ones for the canal undertaking until the Midland Great Western Railway Company purchased it in 1845.

In the 1820s the New Royal Canal Company sought to avail of a government loan scheme to finance the construction of a branch to Longford but the terms imposed were considered unfavourable and the company decided to finance the branch from its own funds. John McMahon, one of the partners in the firm of Henry, Mullins & McMahon, who had built the extension from Coolnahay to the Shannon, resigned his partnership and contracted to build the branch. Not only did he have to contend with great engineering problems, because part of the canal was through boggy terrain, but the local people from **Killashee** and **Richmond Harbour** were strongly opposed to the building of the branch which they saw as a threat to their trade. The canal works were breached several times maliciously and even after the official opening in January 1830 there were further attacks on the canal. The fears of the people were realised, **Longford** became the passenger boat terminus with connecting Bianconi coaches to Sligo, and also the centre for the trade-boats.

Restoration

The remainder of the branch will be dredged as soon as work is completed on the main line. Meanwhile the banks southwards from **Churchlands Bridge** as far as Knockanboy Bridge have been cleared by way of a Social Employment Scheme sponsored by Longford RCAG. Although **Longford Harbour** was filled in over 30 years ago, the site remained unused and unadorned until 1996, when it became a temporary car-park. An indoor swimming pool sits astride the filled-in canal at the entrance to the harbour, but is due to be relocated in a new leisure complex before the turn of the century. There would seem to be no reason, therefore, why the harbour should not be re-excavated, especially as all of the original stonework is in situ under the compacted infill. A new swing bridge would be needed where the railway crossed at low level and there is a problem of a recently built house encroaching on the line of the canal midway between the railway and the harbour. However, as there are only four locks between **Longford** and the **Shannon**, there would appear to be enormous potential for attracting waterborne tourists into an amenity area located in the centre of the town.

Facilities **All Services, Rail and Bus Services:** Longford.

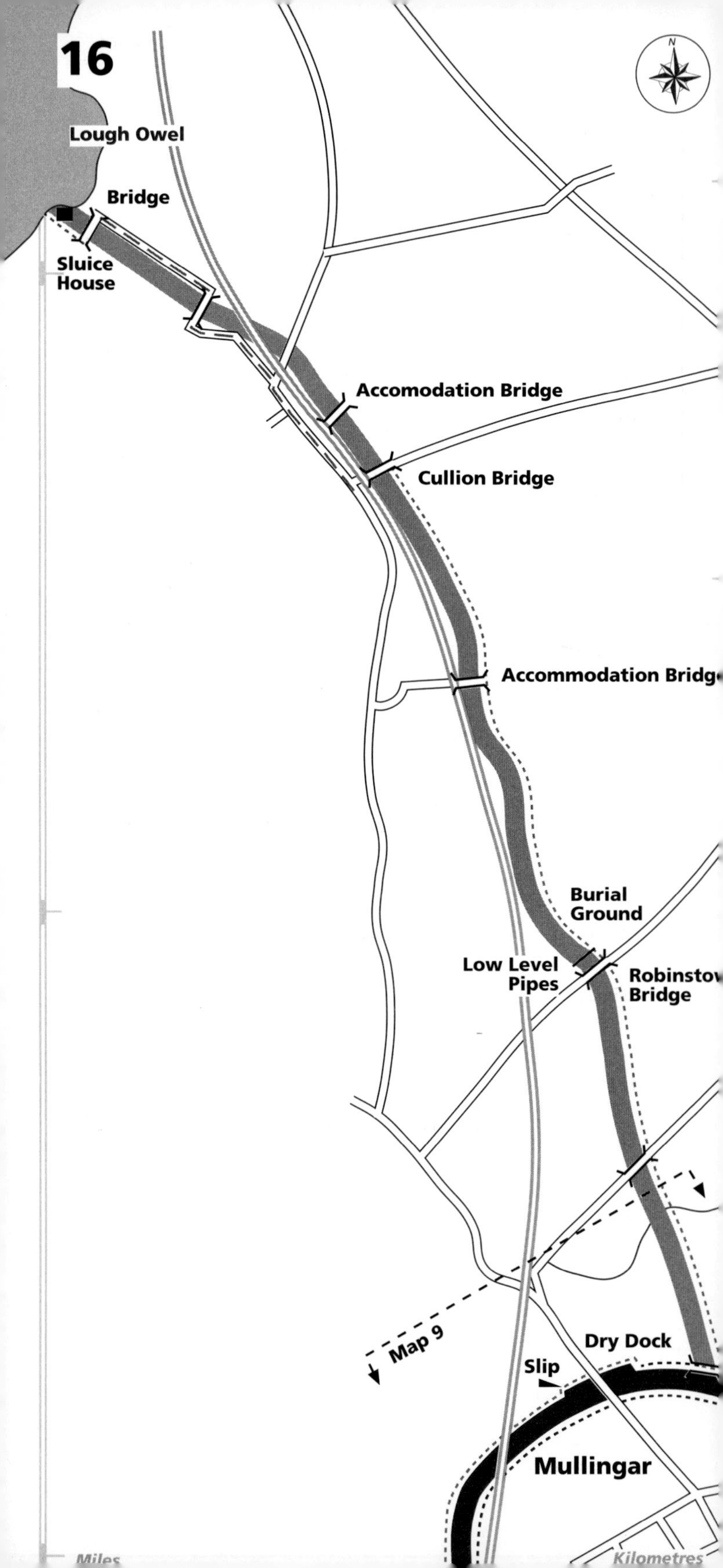

Lough Owel

Bridge

Sluice House

Accomodation Bridge

Cullion Bridge

Accommodation Bridge

Burial Ground

Low Level Pipes

Robinstow Bridge

Dry Dock

Slip

Map 9

Mullingar

Miles

Kilometres

N

THE LOUGH OWEL FEEDER

Lough Owel is the main source of water for the Royal Canal and is connected with the canal via a 2.3mile (3.6 km) channel. This feeder is much narrower and shallower than the canal itself and never formed part of the navigation. At one time, however, it was possible to navigate the feeder channel in a small boat and an account of such a trip, made in 1946, is to be found in **"Green and Silver"** by Tom Rolt who, along with Charles Hadfield and Robert Aickman, founded the Inland Waterways Association in Britain just a few weeks before this trip was made. Such a trip is no longer possible as numerous obstacles now bar the way, but a short journey as far as **Robinstown Bridge** or slightly further is still feasible in a dinghy or canoe.

It is, however, possible to walk alongside the feeder for virtually the whole distance but, as cattle graze the banks, be prepared for muddy conditions and the occasional strands of barbed wire across the route. The path commences on the east side of the beautifully proportioned **towpath bridge** over the mouth of the feeder at **Mullingar harbour**. After a quarter of a mile (400 m) it crosses a tributary of the River Brosna. There is ample headroom under **Robinstown Bridge** but the upstream side is obstructed by a low-level large diameter pipe, under which one could possibly squeeze through in a small dinghy.

The next stretch of bank is not fenced off from adjoining fields and cattle have churned up any path that may once have existed. Keep a look-out for an interesting gateway on the right. A stone lintel carries the inscription **"Mullingar Union"** and the gateway is the entrance into an old burial ground, now just an unkempt field. A short distance further, where the railway line joins the feeder on the west bank, a fence must be crossed before further progress is possible. Whereas the railway follows a gentle curve the feeder takes a winding course and the west bank, between the two, is well wooded.

Beyond the **accommodation bridge** which has lost its parapet walls, the feeder enters a cutting. At **Cullion fish farm** the feeder channel has been culverted by water metering apparatus. The fish farm is licensed to abstract a maximum of 3 million gallons of water per day from **Lough Owel**, via the Royal Canal feeder channel.

At **Cullion Bridge** it is necessary to follow the road for about 500 yards (460 m) (see map), rejoining the feeder channel where it emerges from under the railway line. Close to the lake, and sitting astride the channel, is the **Royal Canal Sluice House**. To the rear of the house can be seen the main sluice gate and the mechanism controlling the flow of water. This was one obstruction which even Rolt and his friends had to portage around! What a pity though that one cannot make a return journey in the way they did when, having transferred the dinghy from **Lough Owel** to the feeder, "we all clambered on board and floated serenely on the current down to the canal, occasionally crouching in the bottom of the boat as we went under a culvert".

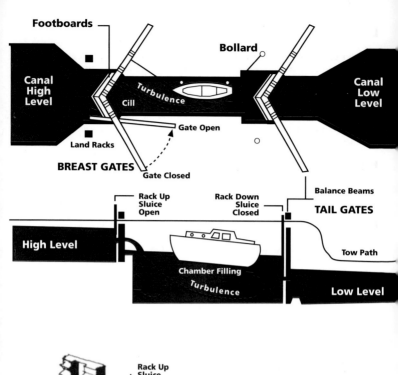

Footboards

Canal High Level

Bollard

Turbulence

Canal Low Level

Cill

Gate Open

Land Racks

BREAST GATES

Gate Closed

Balance Beams

Rack Up Sluice Open

Rack Down Sluice Closed

TAIL GATES

High Level

Tow Path

Chamber Filling

Turbulence

Low Level

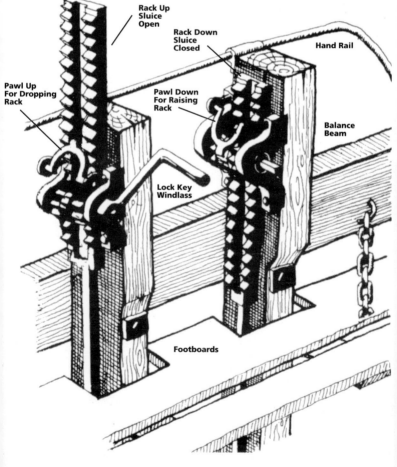

Rack Up Sluice Open

Rack Down Sluice Closed

Hand Rail

Pawl Up For Dropping Rack

Pawl Down For Raising Rack

Balance Beam

Lock Key Windlass

Footboards

LOCKS

To utilise scarce resources most efficiently, there are no lock-keepers on the Royal Canal at present but the Waterways Service have a system whereby maintenance staff are diverted to look after water management and boat movement as necessary. Boatowners interested in putting a boat on the canal should contact the Waterways Service to make the necessary arrangements. The inexperienced should use lock gear extremely cautiously: nothing should be done unless you understand the consequences. In good order, lock racks and gates do not need much force to operate.

Keys   It is necessary to carry your own lock key. It is a crank about 18 in. long with a handle at right angles not less than 10 in. long. A hole 1.25 in. sq. with sides parallel to the handle will fit all rack spindles. Lock keys can be purchased from the Waterways Service.

Descending

Fill the chamber by lowering the tailgate racks and then raising the land racks where fitted and those on the breast gates. When full open the breast gates and move the boat in. A simple ratchet prevents the rack falling when raised. Remove the key - if the ratchet should slip the key would be flung off with some velocity.

Close the breast gates, ensuring that the mitred edges meet cleanly. Lower the land racks and breast racks and open the tail racks, after ensuring that ropes are not tied but looped or hand held and that no part of the boat can catch on a projection as it falls. Particularly keep the rudder clear of the breast gates and of the cill under them.

Ascending

Empty the lock chamber (as for descending), enter, close the tail gates properly after you and lower their racks. Ensure that the boat is well secured bow and stern, with crew ready to shorten the lines as the boat rises. Crew should also watch that no part of the boat is caught under any projection. There is some turbulence when the first breast rack is raised, and the boat will tend to surge forward. It is best to raise the land rack first (if any) or the breast rack on the same side as the boat is tied, so that the surge of water does not tend to push the boat from the wall. Only when the turbulence eases off should a second breast rack be raised.

Leaving Lock

Unless another boat is about to use the lock it is usual to leave it empty, with the racks as you found them.

Difficulties

Gates may jam with rubbish under them or fail to open completely due to rubbish lodging behind them. Re-opening or closing may help.

Man Overboard

Drop all racks at once and make the rescue from the boat. There are no ladders in the lock chambers.

Courtesy

While 'first come first served' is the rule, it is foolish to refuse first passage to a boat coming down if the lock is still full, or vice versa. Enter the lock slowly.

FISHING ON THE ROYAL CANAL

The Waterways Service initiated a five year fish stocking programme in 1991 aimed at upgrading the fishing potential of the canals and turning them into a top class coarse fishery. This has involved fish assessment to quantify existing stocks, tagging fish to determine movement patterns and identifying surplus fish from other sources and transferring these to the canals. In association with this work, the Waterways Service also have a research programme to maintain water quality, with samples taken every two months, and a programme to control weed growth in the water channel. The result of these efforts has been to dramatically improve the fishing potential of the canal and this work will continue as further stretches are restored and water levels controlled. This has led to a noticeable increase in the numbers of organised fishing competitions and in the level of foreign anglers using the canals. Most especially, there has been a significant growth in the number of local residents who fish the canal individually and this is an aspect which the Waterways Service is particularly keen to encourage. Coarse fish to be found in the Royal Canal include Bream, Roach, Rudd, Roach/Bream hybrids, Rudd/Bream hybrids, Tench, Pike and Perch. In selected locations Carp have been stocked. All coarse fishing on the canal must be carried out in accordance with the Fisheries Bye-laws.

SEE ILLUSTRATIONS ON INSIDE BACK COVER

Bream These are a fish which are popular with Irish and English anglers. A shoal fish, they grow on the canal to 6 lb (2.5 kg). They are caught mostly on small red worm or maggot. They can be located by looking at a stretch on a calm evening and detecting the bubbles which they send to the surface. Very light ground-baiting is important to hold the fish in one area. Bream frighten easily in the canal and minimum bank noise is essential if one is to have success.

Rudd These are a lovely golden coloured fish with red fins. A shy fish, they are caught on maggot or bread flake, i.e., fresh bread, lightly pinched on to a small hook. Rudd can be held in one area by throwing light ground bait loosely into the water. When one has caught a few fish, they will often move away. They fish best in the evening near dusk.

Roach These fish resemble Rudd but have slightly red fins and a body with a silver purple tinge. They are prolific breeders and can over-run a system quickly, often resulting in the reduction in size of other species. They feed freely over the whole year and take maggot baits.

Pike There are Pike to 20 lb (9 kg) in the canal but one is more likely to catch fish of 3 to 6 lb (1.5 - 2.5 kg). These fish, common throughout the country, will take dead fish or a spinning bait, such as a spoon or plug.

Perch A common fish which take worm or maggot or even a spinning bait. They are mostly small in the Canal.

Tench A fine scaled fish, brown in colour and with red eyes. A great fighting fish, they grow to specimen size of 6 lb (2.5 kg) and are taken mostly in the evening and early morning with bread, red worm or sweet corn as bait.

Carp These fish are a specialist's fish and are not easily caught by the average angler. They are shy and often require extreme patience to catch with the angler using such strange baits as sausage or meat.

Techniques for Canal Angling

The canal is shallow and in some stretches where the water is clear, angling is difficult during daylight. Extreme caution must be taken to avoid noise or bank disturbances as the fish will detect every move because there is little cover. Light tackle, i.e., line and hooks, is essential for success on the canal. When anglers are seen on the bank, boat users should remember that boat movement will undoubtedly destroy their sport for at least one or two hours. So, please travel slowly past anglers.

WILDLIFE ON THE ROYAL CANAL

Canals are man-made waterways, built some 200 years ago. In the forty five years since commercial trading ceased on the Royal Canal, a series of semi-natural wildlife habitats developed along it. In many areas the towpath and the channel both became overgrown and covered with scrub. The scrub was of two distinct types: on the dry towpath Bramble, Hawthorn, Blackthorn, Guelder-rose, Hazel and Spindle grew; while in the channel were species such as Willow and Alder, which prefer wetter conditions. With the restoration of the Royal Canal to a navigable waterway much of this scrub has been lost. However other canal habitats, which had been choked out by the scrub, have been re-established.

Deep Waterway

Milfoils and Pondweeds grow in the deep water at the centre of the channel. Large numbers of tiny invertebrates, including snails and insect larvae, live in and on these plants. These invertebrates are the food supply for many of the coarse fish found in the canal. Swans and ducks feed on the Yellow Water-lily and the tiny Duckweeds which float on the surface of the water.

Reed Fringe

The reed fringe grows in the shallower water at the edge of the canal. It provides food and shelter for water birds, fish and a range of aquatic invertebrates. Damselflies and dragonflies are often seen patrolling above the reed fringe. Their larvae spend the early part of their lives underwater before climbing up the emergent reeds to shed their skin and fly off as adults. The reed fringe also has an important engineering function: it helps disperse the wave energy caused by wind and boats, and so prevents bank erosion.

Bank

The canal bank between the channel and the towpath is a transitional zone between land and water. Yellow Iris, Marsh Orchids and Cuckooflower are typical bankside plants. The caterpillars of the aptly-named Orange-tip Butterfly feed on the Cuckooflower early in the year.

Grassland

Grassland requires maintenance if it is to be retained as a habitat. In the past, grazing was the most common form of grassland maintenance, but today the canal banks are cut on a regular basis. Cutting once a year allows annual wild flowers to grow and set seed before they are cut, while keeping perennial plants and invading scrub under control. Meadows are valuable habitats, and plants once common in the countryside are still found in the canal grasslands, supporting a range of insects, birds and small mammals.

Boundary Hedgerows

Along most of the length of the canal a hedgerow dominated by Hawthorn grows between the towpath and the surrounding countryside. Hedgerows are valuable wildlife habitats, supporting many birds and small mammals. These depend on the plentiful supply of food: pollen and nectar in spring; fruit and berries in autumn; and the insects living on and in the hedge itself. Spring is the best time to see the flowers of the hedgerow. The white flowers of the Blackthorn appear first, followed by those of Hawthorn and Elder. The ground layer plants including Primroses and Celandines also flower in Spring, before the leaves on the taller trees and shrubs block out the light to the ground.

Stonework

In the past the stone bridges had become overgrown with Ivy and Sycamore, which choked out typical wall plants. With restoration plants such as mosses, ferns and small wild flowers can now be seen again.

Conservation

The Waterways Services is committed to maximising the amenity potential of the canal, catering for the needs of anglers, walkers and wildlife enthusiasts as well as boaters. To this end, the restoration of the Royal Canal is being carried out carefully, taking account of the canal's importance as an environmental resource as well as the engineering requirements of restoration and the demands of modern recreational activities.

CHRONOLOGICAL HISTORY OF THE ROYAL CANAL

1755 Survey made by Thomas Williams and John Cooley for a canal from Dublin to the north Shannon using the rivers Rye Water, Blackwater, Boyne, Deel, Yellow, Lough Derravaragh and the rivers Inny and Camlin.

1756 The more southerly Grand Canal route is chosen by the Commissioners of Inland Navigation.

1789 Aid sought to build a canal from Dublin to Tarmonbarry reviving the old plans. Parliament grants £66,000 to add to the £134,000 promised by subscribers. The charter of the Royal Canal Company enrolled.

1796 Ryewater Aqueduct completed after five years work at a cost of £27,000. Canal opened to Kilcock.

1805 Canal to Thomastown completed. The Grand Canal had been completed to the Shannon in 1804.

1806 Canal completed to Mullingar.

1807 Royal Canal Hotel at Moyvalley opened.

1809 Canal completed to Coolnahay at the western end of the summit level.

1811-13 Company's debt rises to £862,000 despite government grants and loans amounting to £143,856. Parliamentary investigations into the company's affairs and discussions about the line of the canal to the Shannon.

1813 The Royal Canal Company dissolved and the concern handed over to the Directors General of Inland Navigation with instructions to complete the canal at public expense.

1817 Canal completed to the Shannon at Tarmonbarry. Total cost of the canal from Dublin £1,421,954.

1818 The New Royal Canal Company takes over the canal with a government Board of Control to watch over its affairs.

1830 The Longford Branch is opened.

1830s Average annual tonnage carried 80,000 tons and 40,000 passengers.

1845 The entire concern is purchased by the Midland Great Western Railway Company for £298,059 with a view to using the property alongside the canal to lay a railway to the west.

1873 Spencer Dock completed.

1877 Broadstone Harbour filled in as forecourt for the railway terminus.

1880s Average tonnage reduced to 30,000 tons.

1927 Further section of Broadstone Branch filled in. Annual tonnage reduced to 10,000 tons in the 1920s.

1938 Ownership transferred to The Great Southern Railway.

1939-45 Brief revival of trade during the Emergency Years.

1944 Ownership transferred to Coras Iompair Eireann.

1946 L.T.C. Rolt navigated the canal and recorded his trip in 'Green & Silver'.

1951 Last bye-trader, James Leech, of Killucan, ceased to operate.

1955 Douglas Heard's Hark was the last officially recorded boat to pass through the canal, and he made a film of the trip.

1956 The remainder of the Broadstone Branch filled in.

1961 The canal was officially closed to navigation.

1974 The 'Save the Royal Canal' campaign began and the Royal Canal Amenity Group was formed.

1986 Ownership transferred to The Office of Public Works.

1990 46 miles (74 km) restored between 12th Lock and Mullingar.

1996 Ownership transferred to the Department of Arts, Culture and the Gaeltacht.

Distance Table	Miles	Kilometres
Dublin North Wall, lifting bridges and sea lock.		
(Start of Spencer Dock)	0.00	0.00
Sheriff Street drawbridge	0.20	0.30
High level railway bridges	0.55	0.90
Railway loop line, lifting bridge, (End of Spencer Dock)	0.65	1.05
Newcomen Bridge, North Strand Road and lock 1	0.70	1.15
Clarke Bridge, Summerhill Parade	0.85	1.35
Clonliffe Bridge, Russell Street	1.15	1.85
Binns Bridge, Drumcondra Road and lock 2 (double)	1.40	2.25
Lock 3 (double)	1.60	2.55
Lock 4 (double)	1.75	2.80
Junction with Broadstone Branch (now filled in)	1.85	3.00
Westmoreland Bridge, Cross Guns and Lock 5 (double)	1.95	3.15
Lock 6 (double)	2.15	3.45
Railway bridge and Lock 7, Liffey Junction	2.90	4.65
Broome Bridge	3.30	5.30
Reilly's Bridge, Ratoath Road and lock 8	3.65	5.85
Lock 9	4.00	6.45
Longford Bridge, Dublin City-County boundary		
and lock 10 (double)	4.65	7.50
Lock 11 (double)	5.55	8.95
New bridge, Dunsink road	5.80	9.35
Ranelagh Bridge	5.95	9.55
Blanchardstown bypass bridge	6.00	9.65
M 50 Motorway aqueduct	6.05	9.75
Blanchardstown bypass bridge	6.10	9.80
Talbot Bridge and lock 12 (double), Blanchardstown	6.15	9.90
Granard Bridge, Castleknock Road	6.35	10.20
Kirkpatrick Bridge, Carpenterstown	7.30	11.75
Kennan or Neville Bridge, Porterstown	7.85	12.65
Callaghan or Carhampton Bridge, Clonsilla	8.60	13.85
Dublin & Meath Railway Bridge (piers only)	9.15	14.70
Pakenham Bridge, Barberstown	9.40	15.10
Collins Bridge, Coldblow	10.50	16.90
Dublin-Kildare county boundary, boat slip and		
amenity area	11.15	17.95
Cope Bridge	11.70	18.85
Ryewater aqueduct	12.60	20.25
Leixlip Spa and Louisa Bridge	12.85	20.70
Deey Bridge and lock 13	13.85	22.30
Carton Wharf and Pike Bridge	15.00	24.15
Mullen Bridges	16.35	26.30
Maynooth harbour, boat slip and footbridge	16.45	26.45
Bond Bridge	16.75	26.95
Jackson's Bridge and lock 14	17.80	28.65
Bailey's Bridge (accommodation bridge)	18.65	30.00
Chambers Bridge and lock 15, The Maws	19.10	30.75
Kilcock harbour, Shaw's Bridge and lock 16 (double)	20.15	32.40
Allen or Spin Bridge	20.80	33.45
Kildare-Meath county boundary	21.90	35.25
Ryewater feeder, McLoghlin's Bridge and lock 17		
(Ferns or Ferrans lock) (double)	22.50	36.20
Meath-Kildare county boundary	24.65	39.65
Cloncurry Bridge and Kildare-Meath county boundary	26.15	42.10
Enfield Bridge and amenity area	28.05	45.15
Enfield harbour and boat slip	28.15	45.30

River Blackwater aqueduct and Meath-Kildare county boundary	30.35	48.85
Kilmore Bridge	30.85	49.65
Moyvalley Bridges	31.95	51.40
Ribbontail Bridge (footbridge)	33.20	53.40
Kildare-Meath county boundary	33.40	53.75
Harbour and Longwood road aqueduct	34.30	55.20
River Boyne aqueduct	34.45	55.45
Blackshade Bridge	35.80	57.60
Hill of Down or Killyon Bridge	37.35	60.10
Ballasport Bridge	38.15	61.40
Meath-Westmeath county boundary	39.65	63.80
D'Arcy's Bridge	41.80	67.25
Riverstown feeder, Thomastown harbour and bridge and lock 18	42.60	68.55
Lock 19	42.95	69.10
Lock 20	43.20	69.50
Lock 21	43.50	70.00
Riverstown Bridge and lock 22, Killucan	43.75	70.40
Lock 23	44.00	70.80
Lock 24	44.30	71.30
Lock 25 and start of summit level	44.45	71.50
Footy's Bridge	44.55	71.70
Nead's or Heathstown Bridge	45.80	73.70
Lifting accommodation bridge	46.40	74.65
Downs Bridge	47.85	77.00
Footbridge	48.40	77.90
Baltrasna Bridge	50.00	80.45
Feeder	51.00	82.05
Saunders Bridge	52.05	83.75
Harbour (Piper's Boreen)	52.25	84.05
Culverted crossing, site of Dublin road or Moran's Bridge, Mullingar	52.55	84.55
Lough Owel feeder	53.00	85.30
Mullingar harbour, dry dock, low level footbridge, Scanlan's Bridge and boat slip	53.15	85.50
Footbridge (Loreto Convent)	53.25	85.70
Railway Bridge	53.35	85.85
Footbridge	53.50	86.10
The Green Bridge	53.65	86.30
New Bridge (under construction)	54.65	87.95
Footbridge, Mullingar Race Course	54.75	88.10
Kilpatrick Bridge	55.65	89.55
Belmont Bridge	56.50	90.90
Ballinea harbour and Ballinea Bridges	56.90	91.55
Shandonagh Bridge	58.40	93.95
Coolnahay harbour, Lock 26, end of summit level and Dolan Bridge	59.70	96.05
Lock 27	59.95	96.45
Lock 28	60.25	96.95
Walsh's Bridge (accommodation bridge)	60.60	97.50
Kildallan Bridge	61.50	98.95
Lock 29	61.60	99.10
Lock 30	61.80	99.45
Lock 31	61.95	99.70
Lock 32 and Kill Bridge (accommodation bridge)	62.40	100.40
Lock 33	62.75	100.95
Lock 34 and Balroe Bridge	63.50	102.15

Balroe feeder	63.80	102.65
Lock 35, Ballynacargy harbour	64.65	104.00
Ballynacargy Bridge	64.75	104.20
Lock 36 and accommodation bridge	65.65	105.65
Kiddy's Bridge	66.00	106.20
Lock 37 and accommodation bridge	66.40	106.85
Lock 38 and Kelly's Bridge	66.60	107.15
Ledwith's Bridge (accommodation bridge)	66.95	107.70
Blackwater River (passes under canal via 12 ft wide tunnel)	67.50	108.60
Bog Bridge (accommodation bridge)	68.35	110.00
Westmeath-Longford county boundary	68.60	110.40
Quinn's Bridge (accommodation bridge)	69.15	111.25
Whitworth aqueduct over River Inny	69.50	111.85
Scally's Bridge	69.60	112.00
Culverted road crossing, Abbeyshrule	70.05	112.70
Webb's Bridge, Abbeyshrule harbour and boat slip	70.10	112.80
Lock 39 and Draper's Bridge, Tinnelick	71.05	114.30
Allard's Bridge (accommodation bridge)	72.05	115.95
Guy's Bridge (accommodation bridge)	72.75	117.05
Molly Ward's Bridge (accommodation bridge)	73.10	117.60
Fowlard's Bridge	73.75	118.65
Toome Bridge	74.75	120.25
Chaigneau Bridge and Ballybrannigan harbour (near Ballymahon)	75.75	121.90
Culverted road crossing and site of Longford Bridge	76.70	123.40
Archie's Bridge and quay	77.20	124.20
Lock 40 and accommodation bridge, Mullawornia	78.05	125.60
Pake or Tirlicken Bridge and culverted road crossing	78.60	126.45
Foigha harbour and bridge	79.50	127.90
Cloonbreany Bridge (accommodation bridge)	80.50	129.50
Culverted road crossing, Island Bridge and Mosstown harbour, Keenagh	81.65	131.35
Lock 41 and Coolnahinch Bridge (accommodation bridge)	82.55	132.80
Ards Bridge (accommodation bridge)	83.65	134.60
Lock 42, Ards	83.90	135.00
Lyneen or Ballinamore Bridge and culverted road crossing	84.45	135.90
Lower Lyneen or Crossover Bridge	85.15	137.00
Junction with Longford Branch, Cloonsheerin	85.60	137.75
Lock 43 and Aghnaskea Bridge, Killashee	86.45	139.10
Killashee harbour, Lock 44 and Savage Bridge	86.85	139.75
Ballydrum Bridge (accommodation bridge)	87.45	140.70
Culverted road crossing and Begnagh Bridge	88.80	142.90
Bord na Mona culverted crossings	89.70	144.35
Lock 45, Rinnmount	90.00	144.80
Richmond Bridge, Richmond Harbour and dry dock, Cloondara.	90.40	145.45
Lock 46, leading into Camlin River	90.50	145.60

Longford Branch

Distance from Cloonsheerin, junction with Main Line		
Cloonsheerin Bridge (accommodation bridge)	0.20	0.30
Aghantrah Bridge	1.00	1.60
Newtown Bridge (accommodation bridge)	1.90	3.05
Cloonturk Bridge (accommodation bridge)	2.60	4.20
Knockanboy Bridge and culverted road crossing	3.00	4.85
Culverted road crossing and Churchlands Bridge	3.60	5.80
Farranyoogan Bridge (accommodation bridge)	4.40	7.10
New terminus south of railway	5.20	8.35

WATERWAYS SERVICE

The Waterways Service of the Department of Arts, Culture and the Gaeltacht is responsible for the maintenance of over 700 kilometres of our inland waterways. This extensive network is made up of navigable rivers, lakes and canals.

Our inland waterways, built or improved in the 18th and 19th centuries for commercial transport, are today used for a variety of recreational pursuits - boating (of course!) in a range of large and small boats, from rowing boats to yachts to cruisers of all sizes; fishing; and walking - and are enjoyed by all who appreciate nature, local history and industrial archaeology.

Royal Canal

The Royal Canal was closed to navigation in 1961. Over the years the canal silted up and dried out; channel, banks and towpath were all hidden under a tangle of vegetation; and low bridges were built over the once-busy waterway, a concrete reminder that navigation was not seen as an option for the future. Restoration of the Royal Canal, initiated by the Inland Waterways Association of Ireland and the Royal Canal Amenity Group, has been carried on by first OPW and then the Waterways Service since 1987. By 1994 over half the canal was again navigable, with further stretches in water and restoration work proceeding westwards.

The canal is being developed for more than just boating - the heavily overgrown towpath has been opened up for walkers, and a fisheries development programme is being carried out. An ecological survey was done, and nature conservation principles have been incorporated into maintenance works. The public amenity role of the canal is promoted and protected at all times.

Grand Canal

When the Grand Canal was transferred to The Office of Public Works in 1986 (with the Royal Canal and the Barrow Navigation) the fabric of the system was in very poor condition. Since then considerable effort has been made in upgrading the canal. Major repairs have been carried out to the bog embankments to safeguard these sections, and this work will continue for many years. Most lock-gates have now been replaced, dredging has been undertaken, moorings provided, water supplies augmented and weed control greatly improved. Overall, a higher level of maintenance has been achieved. A companion volume to this guide, A Guide to the Grand Canal, is available.

Barrow Navigation

This is widely considered to be the most picturesque of all Irish waterways. It is being upgraded by the Waterways Service - ongoing works include the replacement of lock-gates, dredging of the channel, provision of slips and mooring facilities, and making the towpath more accessible for walkers. A guide to the navigation and trackway is available.

Shannon Navigation

The Shannon Navigation has been the responsibility of the State since the middle of the last century. Over the last three decades facilities for boating traffic have been greatly improved with the provision of new quays, jetties and harbours; upgrading of the locks; and the opening of new destinations (Lough Allen via the Lough Allen Canal, and the Erne Navigation through the Shannon-Erne Waterway). Further extensions are being planned, including the construction of a new navigation on the River Suck to Ballinasloe. Navigation charts for the Shannon Navigation are available.

Shannon-Erne Waterway

This link between the Shannon and the Erne (formerly called the Ballinamore and Ballyconnell Canal) was re-opened in 1994 following over a century of dereliction. In that year over 3,000 boats passed along the restored waterway - two hundred times more than used it during the nine years that it was opened for commercial traffic (1860-9). Navigation charts for this waterway have been published.

THE INLAND WATERWAYS ASSOCIATION OF IRELAND

The IWAI was formed in 1954 to promote the development, use and maintenance of Ireland's navigable rivers, lakes and canals. When the Shannon was almost totally undeveloped for pleasure boating, the IWAI fought the building of low bridges thus ensuring the survival of the river as a national tourism asset. Later the IWAI resisted the threatened closure of the Grand Canal in Dublin and campaigned successfully for the restoration of the Royal Canal.

Improvement and Restoration
Nowadays the activities of the IWAI are on a larger scale. It focuses public interest on the little-known Barrow Navigation, now beginning to welcome commercial boat hiring. It has successfully campaigned for the re-opening of the Lough Allen Canal, thus extending the Shannon Navigation northwards, and for the restoration of the Ballinamore and Ballyconnell Canal which re-opened in 1994 and once again connects the Shannon with Lough Erne.

In 1990 a campaign was commenced to restore the Ulster Canal, another cross-border waterway, linking the Erne to Lough Neagh via Clones, Smithborough, Monaghan, Middletown, Caledon, Benburb, Blackwatertown and Charlemont. Although only half the length of the Royal Canal, because it has been closed for over 60 years the task of restoration will be of a similar magnitude.

Rallies
The Association organises annual rallies on the Barrow, Corrib, Erne, Grand Canal, Shannon and Slaney and many other events and festivals. Competitions help to raise standards of boatmanship and seaworthiness.

Social Events
Film shows, lectures and social occasions help to bring together waterways users out of season.

Newsletter
Inland Waterways News, published quarterly, goes to every member of the Association and brings local activities and developments into perspective. Some branches of the association publish local newsletters.

Restoration Projects
The IWAI organises work parties and raises funds to improve navigations and to restore derelict ones.

Branches and Membership
The IWAI is made up of the following branches: Athlone, Barrow, Belturbet, Boyne, Carrick-on-Shannon, Corrib, Dublin, Kildare, Lough Derg, North Barrow, Northern Ireland, Offaly, Shannon Harbour and Slaney, all represented on a national council. The annual subscription is £12 and the address of the branch secretaries may be obtained from: IWAI, Stone Cottage, Claremont Road, Killiney, Co. Dublin.

THE ROYAL CANAL AMENITY GROUP

Formed as a local organisation in 1974, the original objective of the RCAG was to promote and participate in the development of the full amenity potential of the Royal Canal in County Dublin. From these small beginnings the group continued to grow and now has a membership of approximately 500. It was not long before the group's activities extended eastwards into the City and westwards into Kildare and Meath, and very soon it had assumed 'responsibility' for the whole canal. The formation of local branches was encouraged: the first in Ballynacargy & Abbeyshrule, then in Kilcock, Enfield, Killucan, Maynooth, Mullingar, Leixlip and Longwood, and later in Keenagh & Foigha, Killashee, Ballymahon, Longford and Cloondara. All these branches work closely with community councils or residents associations to restore and develop local stretches of the waterway.

Much of the group's work is done voluntarily by members, but it also sponsors many Youth and Social Employment Schemes. One of the most successful of these was a joint RCAG/FAS project for the construction of new lock gates for the whole Dublin-Kildare-Meath stretch of the canal. The group, of course, works in close collaboration with the staff of the Waterways Service who provide invaluable help and assistance.

We need your help

Although, in the past, the RCAG has received financial assistance from local authorities and other bodies it is now almost entirely dependent upon membership subscriptions, donations and profits from fund-raising activities to meet the considerable costs involved. Having, with the aid of this guide, viewed at first hand the results of the group's work we feel certain that you will wish to be more closely associated with it. You may like to make a donation, or join the group as either an annual or life member. Members receive a regular newsletter and they have an opportunity to meet together at film shows, canal walks, boat rallies and other social events. Needless to say, your help at work parties is always welcome but is not obligatory!

How to join

The Honorary Membership Secretary, Noel McGeeney, Canal Harbour, Longford will be pleased to send you a membership application form and, if requested, the name and address of the Secretary of your nearest branch.

Work Parties and Other Activities

Further information on work parties, boat rallies and other activities is obtainable from the Honorary Secretary, Paddy Greene, Killucan, Co. Westmeath.

© Government of Ireland 1997

BAILE ÁTHA CLIATH:
ARNA FHOILSIÚ AG OIFIG AN tSOLÁTHAIR.

Le ceannach díreach ón
OIFIG DHÍOLTA FOILSEACHÁN RIALTAIS,
TEACH SUN ALLIANCE, SRÁID THEACH LAIGHEAN,
BAILE ÁTHA CLIATH 2,
nó trí aon díoltóir leabhar.

DUBLIN:
PUBLISHED BY THE STATIONERY OFFICE.

To be purchased through any Bookseller, or directly from the
GOVERNMENT PUBLICATIONS SALE OFFICE,
SUN ALLIANCE HOUSE, MOLESWORTH STREET, DUBLIN 2.

Price: £5.00